# DOG BREEDS FOR KIDS

# A Children's Picture Book About Dog Breeds

A Great Simple Picture Book for Kids to Learn about Different Dog Breeds

Melissa Ackerman

PUBLISHED BY:

Melissa Ackerman

Copyright © 2016

*All rights reserved.*

*No part of this publication may be copied, reproduced in any format, by any means, electronic or otherwise, without prior consent from the copyright owner and publisher of this book.*

*Disclaimer*

*The information contained in this book is for general information purposes only. The information is provided by the authors and while we endeavor to keep the information up to date and correct, we make no representations or warranties of any kind, express or implied, about the completeness, accuracy, reliability, suitability or availability with respect to the book or the information, products, services, or related graphics contained in the book for any purpose. Any reliance you place on such information is therefore strictly at your own risk.*

# TABLE OF CONTENTS

Affenpinscher ............................................................................................................... 7

Afghan Hound .............................................................................................................. 8

Airedale Terrier ............................................................................................................ 9

Akbash ........................................................................................................................ 10

Akita Inu ..................................................................................................................... 11

Alaskan Klee Kai ........................................................................................................ 12

Alaskan Malamute ...................................................................................................... 13

American Bulldog ....................................................................................................... 14

American Cocker Spaniel .......................................................................................... 15

American Eskimo Dog ............................................................................................... 16

American Foxhound ................................................................................................... 17

American Staffordshire Terrier ................................................................................. 18

American Water Spaniel ............................................................................................ 19

Anatolian Shepherd Dog ............................................................................................ 20

Australian Shepherd ................................................................................................... 21

Australian Silky Terrier .............................................................................................. 22

Barbet .......................................................................................................................... 23

Basenji ......................................................................................................................... 24

Basset Hound .............................................................................................................. 25

Bavarian Mountain Hound ........................................................................................ 26

Beagle .......................................................................................................................... 27

Bearded Collie ............................................................................................................ 28

Bedlington Terrier ...................................................................................................... 29

Belgian Shepherd Dog (Groenendael) ...................................................................... 30

Bergamasco Shepherd ................................................................................................ 31

Berger Blanc Suisse .................................................................................................... 32

Black Russian Terrier ................................................................................................. 33

Bloodhound ................................................................................................................ 34

Bolognese .................................................................................................................... 35

Border Collie .............................................................................................................. 36

Boston Terrier ............................................................................................................. 37

Boxer ........................................................................................................................... 38

| | |
|---|---|
| Bulldog | 39 |
| Cairn Terrier | 40 |
| Canadian Eskimo Dog | 41 |
| Catalan Sheepdog | 42 |
| Cavalier King Charles Spaniel | 43 |
| Cesky Terrier | 44 |
| Chihuahua | 45 |
| Chow Chow | 46 |
| Dachshund | 47 |
| Dalmatian | 48 |
| Dandie Dinmont Terrier | 49 |
| Doberman Pinscher | 50 |
| English Cocker Spaniel | 51 |
| English Setter | 52 |
| English Springer Spaniel | 53 |
| Field Spaniel | 54 |
| Finnish Spitz | 55 |
| French Bulldog | 56 |
| German Pinscher | 57 |
| German Shepherd Dog | 58 |
| Giant Schnauzer | 59 |
| Golden Retriever | 60 |
| Great Dane | 61 |
| Greater Swiss Mountain Dog | 62 |
| Greenland Dog | 63 |
| Havanese | 64 |
| Ibizan Hound | 65 |
| Irish Wolfhound | 66 |
| Italian Greyhound | 67 |
| Jack Russell Terrier | 68 |
| Japanese Chin | 69 |
| Japanese Spitz | 70 |
| Karelian Bear Dog | 71 |
| Keeshond | 72 |

| Breed | Page |
|---|---|
| Komondor | 73 |
| Kuvasz | 74 |
| Labrador Retriever | 75 |
| Lhasa Apso | 76 |
| Maltese | 77 |
| Norwich Terrier | 78 |
| Otterhound | 79 |
| Papillon | 80 |
| Pekingese | 81 |
| Pomeranian | 82 |
| Poodle | 83 |
| Pug | 84 |
| Puli | 85 |
| Pumi | 86 |
| Pyrenean Mastiff | 87 |
| Rhodesian Ridgeback | 88 |
| Rottweiler | 89 |
| Saluki | 90 |
| Samoyed | 91 |
| Scottish Deerhound | 92 |
| Shar Pei | 93 |
| Shih Tzu | 94 |
| Siberian Husky | 95 |
| Silken Windhound | 96 |
| St. Bernard | 97 |
| Standard Schnauzer | 98 |
| Tibetan Spaniel | 99 |
| Toy Fox Terrier | 100 |
| Welsh Terrier | 101 |
| West Highland White Terrier | 102 |
| Whippet | 103 |
| White Shepherd | 104 |
| Wirehaired Vizsla | 105 |
| Yorkshire Terrier | 106 |

# Affenpinscher

Affenpinschers are also known as Monkey Terrier. They usually weigh around 6.5 to 13.2 pounds and stands 9 to 12 inches tall. It has a notable monkey-like face expression and shaggy coat in black, grey, silver, red, tan, and beige colors. However, black Affenpinschers are more preferred. They are active, adventurous, curious, and stubborn dogs. They are also fun-loving and playful, lively, affectionate and protective towards family members. Affenpinschers are not recommended for homes with children due to their territorial behavior when it comes to their toys and food.

# Afghan Hound

Afghan Hounds are dogs with extremely long, thick, fine and silky coat that requires care and grooming. Their tail has a ring curl at the end. They are also tall, around 61–74 cm in height and weight at about 20–27 kg. Their coat may be in any color. Most of Afghan Hounds have a black facial mask or black markings that give a mask appearance on their face. Afghan Hounds can be aloof but happy, active and clownish when they're playing. They also may not get along with small animals.

# Airedale Terrier

Airedale Terriers are also called Bingley Terriers and Waterside Terriers. Traditionally, they are called "King of Terriers" because they are the largest breed of terrier. Terriers are small, very active and fearless dogs with stiff hair. Airedale Terriers' medium-length hard coat is black and tan in color. Usually, their weight is around 20–30 kg and height at about 58–61 cm for males, with females slightly smaller. Airedale Terriers are also used as war dogs, guide dogs and police dogs. They are an alert and energetic breed,

# Akbash

Akbash Dogs are large dogs native to western Turkey. They are considered as one of the national dog breeds of Turkey. They are also used as livestock guardian dogs or shepherd dogs that look after the sheep and other livestock. Akbash Dogs have smooth short to medium white coat, long legs and curly tail. Under their white coat, their skin is pinkish in color with black or blackish-brown blotches. They also have black or blackish-brown eye rims, nose and lips. Their personality are said to be calm and aware, not shy nor aggressive. As a protection dog, they are quite suspicious towards strangers and unusual sounds or changes in their territory.

# Akita Inu

Akita Inu is a large breed of dog also known as Akita Ken and Japanese Akita. They originate from the mountainous northern regions of Japan. They have a short coat, large, bear-like head, triangular ears. Their tails are carried over the top of their back in a gentle or double curl. When it comes to coat color, they may be red, fawn (light yellowish tan), sesame (very light brown), brindle (tiger-striped) or pure white. All coat colors come with "Urajiro" markings. Urajiro is characterized by whitish coat on the sides of the nose and mouth part, on the cheeks, on the underside and on the inside of the legs. The Akita Inu is a powerful, independent and dominant dog. They are also aloof with strangers but affectionate with family members. They are best known worldwide from the true story of Hachikō, a loyal dog who lived in Japan before World War II.

# Alaskan Klee Kai

Alaskan Klee Kai is a spitz type dog that resembles the Alaskan Husky, a dog used for sled racing. Spitz type dogs are known for their long and thick fur, pointed ears and nose and tail that often curls over their back. They are also small to medium-sized dogs that measures 13 to 15 inches in height and weigh between 9.9 and 15 pounds. Alaskan Klee Kai also comes in three color including black and white, gray and white and red and white. They are quiet, energetic and highly intelligent dogs with an average life expectancy of 12 to 16 years. They are also playful, curious and cautious around unfamiliar individuals.

# Alaskan Malamute

Alaskan Malamutes are large domestic dogs developed for moving heavy cargo because of their strength and endurance. Their coarse coat that stands off the body comes in various shades of gray and white, sable and white, black and white, seal and white, red and white, or solid white. They also have a strong body, small, erect ears and almond-shaped eyes in different shades of brown. Their tail should be well furred and is curled over their back. Alaskan Malamutes are also very fond of people and have love for snow.

# American Bulldog

American Bulldogs are a breed of working dog. Working dogs are dogs that learn and perform tasks to assist and entertain their human companions. They have a stocky body, with a large head and short, smooth coat. Their color ranges from predominantly white with patches of red or black, or brindle (tiger-striped). They may also be in black, red, brown and fawn colors. They should also have black or pink pigmentation on their nose and eye rims. When it comes to eye color, American Bulldogs' eyes are usually brown. They are also confident, social, and active dogs that drools a lot.

# American Cocker Spaniel

American Cocker Spaniels are a breed of sporting dog. Sporting dogs are used for hunting. They are considered as the smallest sporting dog. They have an average height between 13.5 and 15.5 inches. They are also dogs of normal proportions (normal head, legs and tail size). They also have medium long silky fur on their body and ears. This fur hangs down on their legs and belly. Their ears are also long and dropped and are not erect like other dogs. They also have dark, large and rounded eyes and black or brown nose. The coat of American Cocker Spaniels come in a variety of shades of colors like black, black and tan, light cream and dark red.

# American Eskimo Dog

American Eskimo Dogs are a breed of companion dog that come from Germany. Companion dogs usually do not work, providing only companionship as a pet. However, aside from being a watchdog and companion, they also become popular in the United States as a circus performer. In appearance, American Eskimo Dogs are small to medium in size with straight and long fur in white, or white with cream. They also have erect triangular ears, and black lips, nose, and eye rims. Additionally, they are affectionate, loving dogs that are easy to train and with high intelligence.

# American Foxhound

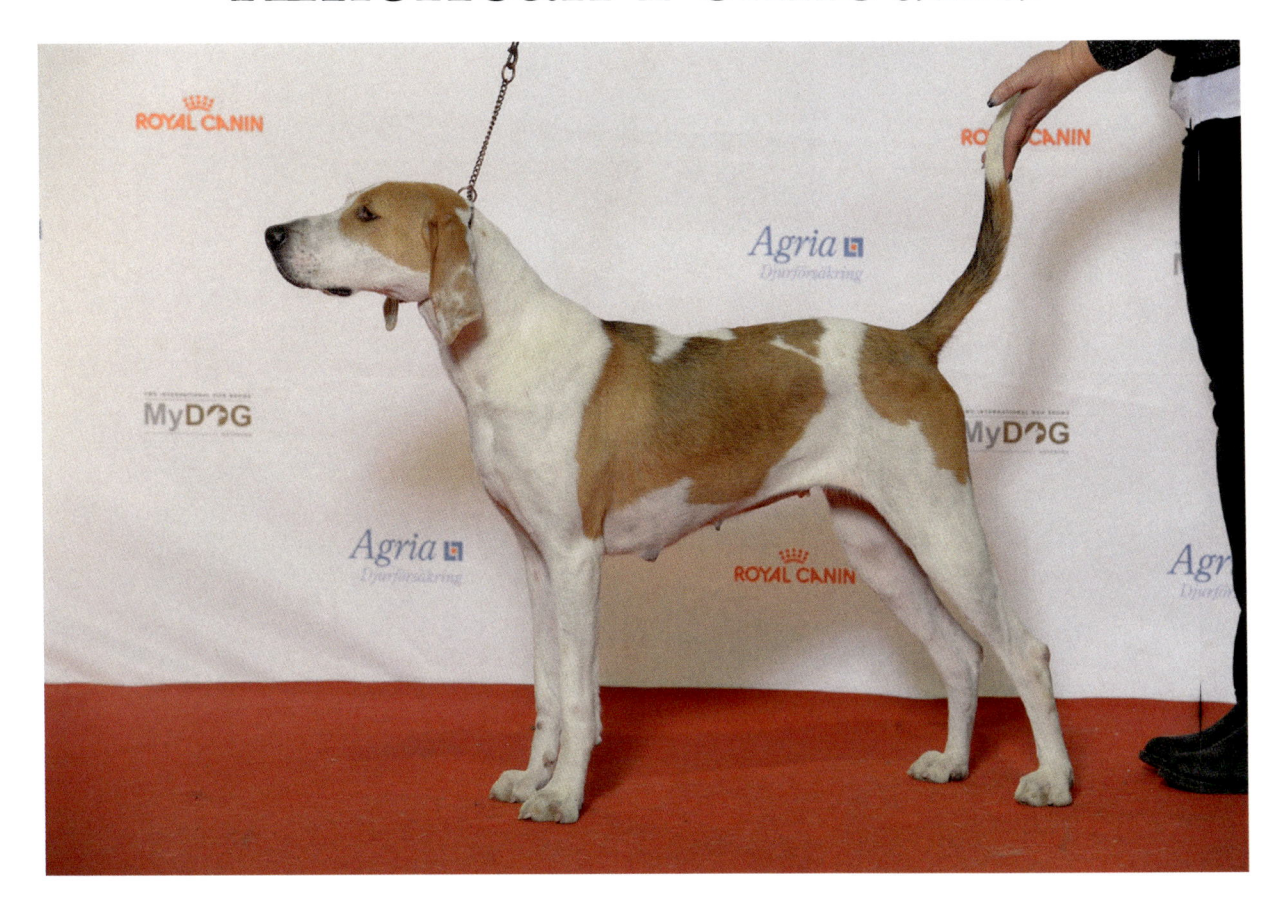

American Foxhound is a rare breed of dog considered as scent hounds. Scent hounds are hounds or dogs that hunt by scent rather than by sight. They have a medium length hard coat that comes in any color. They are also tall dogs with long ears, large eyes, straight nose, fox-like feet, and a slightly curved tail. American Foxhounds are also known to have a musical bark when hunting. They are also said to be sweet-natured, gentle, easygoing, and gets along with children and other animals.

# American Staffordshire Terrier

American Staffordshire Terriers are also known as Amstaff or Stafford. They are medium in size and have a thick and short coat in all colors. They have a muscular body and powerful head. Additionally, they have a medium length nose, dark and round eyes and a short tail. When it comes to behavior, American Staffordshire Terriers are people-oriented dog, friendly, and are loyal to his own family.

# American Water Spaniel

American Water Spaniel is a hunting dog developed in the state of Wisconsin during the 19th century. They are medium-sized dog with tightly curled or slightly wavy coat that comes in different shades of brown. Their coat also has an oily feel, which gives off a "doggy smell". Their average height is around 15–18 inches, while their average weight around 25–45 pounds. The color of their eyes may be in any color except yellow. Some of their characteristics also include broad skull and long, wide ears. They also are quite vocal, often bond with one particular individual and enjoy being the center of attention.

# Anatolian Shepherd Dog

Anatolian Shepherd Dogs are dogs which originated in Anatolia. They are large and very strong dogs, with excellent sight and hearing. They have a muscular body, thick necks and broad heads. They also have triangular ears that hang down and thick coat that comes in any color. However, their most common colors are white cream, light brown and white with large spots. Anatolian Shepherd Dogs are independent and responsible dogs that guard their owner's livestock animals. They are also intelligent and can learn quickly, though, might prefer not to obey.

# Australian Shepherd

Australian Shepherds or Aussies are medium-sized dogs developed in the ranches of western United States. Their coat may be in black, red, blue and red merle (marbled red, white and buff). Merle refers to a pattern in a dog's coat that shows patches of dark and light areas. They may also have copper or white fur on their face, chest, and legs. The Australian Shepherd's eye color may be of any shade of brown or blue. They may also have two different colored eyes or "split eyes" (a half-brown, half-blue eye). Additionally, Australian Shepherds have a long tail and kind, loving, and loyal personality.

# Australian Silky Terrier

Australian Silky Terriers are small dogs developed in Australia. They have short legs and long silky grey and white or blue and tan coat. Their coat also hangs straight and is parted along their back. To maintain the silkiness of their coat, they should be groomed and shampooed regularly. Australian Silky Terriers are rather longer than tall. They also have triangular head, small almond-shaped eyes and small but erect ears. Behavior wise, Australian Silky Terriers are alert and active. They also enjoy running, brisk walking and playing ball.

# Barbet

Barbets are rare medium-sized water dogs. Water dogs are those that help in hunting in water. Their "barbet" comes from the French word *barbe*, which means beard. Obviously, they have a pronounced beard. Their long and curly hair comes in pure black, brown, fawn, grey, pale fawn or white. Grey and white are extremely rare while the most common colors are black or brown with white markings on the chest, chin, paw and legs. They also have medium-sized legs, tail and head with dropped ears and round eyes. Barbets are also described as friendly, joyful, obedient, intelligent and great with children, families, and the elderly.

# Basenji

Basenji is a type of hunting dog. They are small, short-haired dogs with upright ears, curled tail and wrinkled forehead. Their eyes are almond-shaped. They are also considered as square breed, meaning, their length is proportion or equals to their height. They come in different colors like red, black, tricolor (have three different colors), brindle (tiger-striped), and the rare *trundle* (tricolor with brindle points). Basenjis also have white feet, chests and tail tips. They are also athletic, powerful, alert, curious, and reserved with strangers. They have a tendency to not get along with other dogs. They also do not like wet weather.

# Basset Hound

Basset Hounds are short-legged dogs. They are scent hounds or dogs the hunt using their sense of smell. Their name *Basset* is from the French word *bas* and suffix *-et*, meaning "rather low". Despite their short legs, Basset Hounds are large and long. They are also quite heavy for their size. The hanging skin on their face causes them to occasionally look sad. Additionally, Basset Hounds have neck which is wider than their head. And because they are heavy and have such short legs, they cannot hold themselves above water for very long. The coat of a Basset is medium-short, smooth and hard that usually come in the classic tri-color pattern of black, tan, and white. However, they can also be in white coat with red spots, red coat with white feet and tail or lemon and white. Many of them have white tip to their tail. They are also described as friendly, outgoing, and playful dog that goes along with children and other pets.

# Bavarian Mountain Hound

Bavarian Mountain Hounds are scent hounds from Germany. They have a strong, elongated head and lips covering their mouth. They also have a black or dark red nose with wide nostrils. Their medium-sized ears hang against their head. When it comes to their body, Bavarian Mountain Hounds are a bit longer than they are tall. Their coat is short, thick and shiny that comes in all shades of fawn (with black mask or black markings on the face) or brindle (tiger-striped). Bavarian Mountain Hounds are also said to be calm, quiet, poised, and attached to their masters and family.

# Beagle

Beagles are small-sized dogs primarily developed to hunt hare. They have an excellent sense of smell and tracking instinct. They have been used as detection dogs for illegal agricultural imports and foodstuffs around the world. They also have broad head, short square-cut nose and short legs. Their eyes are large and come in hazel or brown color. Their ears are long and large and hang down their cheeks. They also have a long tail tipped with white, muscular body and a medium-length coat that comes in tricolor or bicolor. The most common however, is a tricolored Beagle in white with large black areas and light brown shading. Snoopy of the comic strip *Peanuts* has been considered as "the world's most famous beagle". They are also popular as pets due to their size and good temper.

# Bearded Collie

Bearded Collies or Beardies are dogs once used by Scottish shepherds in herding sheep. But these days, they are more popular as family companion. They are medium-sized dogs with long and lean body, large head and large square-shaped black nose. They also have medium-sized ears covered with hair that hang close to their head. Their tail also hangs down except when they are excited. They have a shaggy, waterproof, coat that hangs over their entire body including the chin that comes in light gray or cream colors with or without white markings. Bearded Collies are also regarded as cheerful, happy-go-lucky dogs that are affectionate, playful and are perfect companions for children.

# Bedlington Terrier

Bedlington Terriers are small dogs that resemble a lamb. Their shaggy, hard and rugged coat comes in blue, red or sandy coloration. However, due to their graying gene, Bedlington Terrier puppies are born with black or dark brown fur which lighten to grey or red as they mature. They also have a rounded head, small almond-shaped eyes, and an arched back. The body should also be slightly longer in length than in height. Bedlington Terriers are good with children. They also have powerful swimming skills and are noted for being quick and having high endurance.

# Belgian Shepherd Dog (Groenendael)

Groenendaels are dogs that are also called the Belgian Sheepdog. They are medium in size, hard-working and have a square proportion (length and height is proportion or equal). They are also strong and athletic in appearance. The top of their skull is somewhat flattened rather than rounded. Additionally, they have almond-shaped eyes in brown color, upright triangular ears and straight and strong legs. Their thick and hard coat is always black in color which may have small white markings on the chest. Groenendaels are also intelligent, active, loyal and quite affectionate dogs.

# Bergamasco Shepherd

Bergamasco Shepherds are dogs originally used as herding dogs. Herding dogs are dogs that are trained in herding or maintaining a group or herd of animals and move them from place to place. Bergamasco Shepherds have a muscular body, large head and a thick tail. Their entire body is covered with plenty of coat that forms mats. Their very unique coat form flocks, meaning, strands of hair are weaved together creating flat mats that protects them from weather and predators. Typically, the hair on their head is long and hangs over their eyes. Their coat color can be gray or black. Shadings of pale cream-brown and fawn may also appear at the lower part of their coat as a result of discoloration. When it comes to their personality, Bergamasco Shepherds are alert, observant and patient dogs suited as guard and companion dog.

# Berger Blanc Suisse

Berger Blanc Suisse or White Swiss Shepherd is a breed of medium-sized dog from Switzerland. They have a straight (sometimes slightly wavy) medium-length coat of pure white hair. They also have a muscular body, erect ears, and a low-set medium-length tail. They are slightly longer in length than in height. They are also gentle, very intelligent and can learn easily. They are loyal to their family but, may be wary around strangers,

# Black Russian Terrier

Black Russian Terriers are also known as the Tchiorny Terrier. The word *tchiorny* is the Russian word for black. Their coat is coarse, hard and thick and comes in is black or black with some gray hairs. They also have a beard and thick eyebrows. They are also slightly longer than tall, with males being larger than females. They have a large, strong and muscular body. They also have a large black nose, full, rounded and black lips, medium-sized dark eyes and triangular ears. The Russian Black Terriers are calm, confident, courageous, and highly intelligent dogs.

# Bloodhound

Bloodhounds are large scent hounds or dogs that hunt using their sense of smell. They are originally bred to hunt deer, wild boar and for tracking people. They are also being used by police all over the world to track escaped prisoners, missing people, lost children and lost pets. Their hard fur may come in colors like black, tan and red. They also have a long head, long and black nose and diamond-shaped eyes in hazel to yellow colors Additionally, Bloodhounds have soft, drooping ears and a lot of extra, wrinkled skin, especially around their head and neck. Bloodhounds are gentle, tireless, affectionate and even-tempered with humans, making them excellent family pets. However, like other pets, they require supervision when around small children.

# Bolognese

Bolognese is a small type of dog that originates in Italy. They are considered as companion dogs that love attention, and are excellent house pets. They have a distinctive short, wooly white coat, square build, black lips and dark round eyes. They also have long hanging ears and a curved tail. When it comes to their personality, Bolognese dogs are playful, easygoing, intelligent and loyal. However, they are more reserved and not hyperactive.

# Border Collie

Border Collies are herding dogs especially used to herd sheep. They are noted for their high intelligence and obedience. In fact, they are often referred to as the most intelligent of all domestic dogs. They are medium-sized dogs with a thick coat that comes in many colors but the most common are black and white combination, black tricolor (black/tan/white), red and white, and red tricolor (red/tan/white). Moreover, Borders Collies have oval eyes in brown or blue colors and upright or dropped ears. They are also slightly longer than taller.

# Boston Terrier

Boston Terriers are dogs that originated in the United States. They have short coat in black, brindle (tiger striped) or seal with white markings. They are well-proportioned dogs that are small in size and with short tail, upright ears and square-shaped head. They are also said to be highly intelligent and easy to train. They are also friendly but can be stubborn sometimes.

# Boxer

Boxer dogs are medium-sized, short-haired dogs from Germany. Their coat is smooth and comes in many colors like white, fawn, mahogany, black or brindled (tiger-striped), all with or without white markings. They also have broad, short skull, very strong jaw, and a powerful bite. Furthermore, Boxer dogs have large black nose, dark brown eyes, ears that are set high on their head and straight front legs. They are also happy, high-spirited, playful, curious and energetic dogs with high intelligence and willingness to learn.

# Bulldog

Bulldogs are medium-sized dogs usually referred to as the English Bulldogs or British Bulldogs. They have a muscular body, wrinkled face and a unique pushed-in nose. They also have a wide head and shoulders, thick folds of skin on their brow and round, black eyes. Moreover, Bulldogs have a short, straight tail and short, flat coat in red, fawn, white, brindle, and piebald (colored spots on a white background) colors. Generally, they are also noted for getting along well with children, other dogs, and pets and for being very attached to their home and family.

# Cairn Terrier

Cairn Terriers are one of the oldest terrier breeds. Terrier breeds are dogs that are small, wiry, active and fearless dogs. They have a weather-resistant shaggy coat that comes in black, cream, red, sandy, gray, or brindled (tiger-striped) colors. Their most notable characteristic, however, is the ability of brindled Cairns to frequently change color throughout their lifetime or become more black or silver as they age. They also have a fox-like expression, broad head, black nose and hazel-colored eyes and erect ears. Cairn Terriers are also alert, loyal, curious, cheerful, lovable and friendly. They love playing with children as well.

# Canadian Eskimo Dog

Canadian Eskimo Dogs are also called as *qimmiq* or *qimmit*. Currently, they are threatened with extinction with a 2008 estimate of only 300 purebred dogs. They have athletic build, triangular ears and thick-feathered tail carried over their back. Their thick coat can be in almost any color. However, pure silver, black and white dogs are common as well as white dogs with colored patches. Canadian Eskimo Dogs are also loyal, tough, brave, intelligent, alert, affectionate and gentle,

# Catalan Sheepdog

Catalan Sheepdogs are companion dogs from Europe. They are usually used for herding and guarding livestock animals. Their coat is long and comes in different shades of fawn to dark sable and light to dark grey. They have a medium built and a head with a beard, moustache and eyebrows. Their tail, as well as their legs is covered with hair. Catalan Sheepdogs are also intelligent, easy to train, cheerful and courageous.

# Cavalier King Charles Spaniel

Cavalier King Charles Spaniels are small spaniels that originated in the United Kingdom. They are considered as one of the most popular breeds in many countries. Spaniels are dogs that help hunters find, hunt and retrieve birds. They have a medium length, silky, smooth coat in blenheim (chestnut and white), tricolor (black/white/tan), black and tan, and ruby colors. They also have long hairs on their ears, feet, legs and tail. Cavalier King Charles Spaniels are also well-proportioned little dog with slightly rounded head, full muzzle (nose and mouth part), black nose, round, dark brown eyes and long ears. They are generally friendly, affectionate and good with both children and other animals.

# Cesky Terrier

Cesky Terriers are small dogs from Czechoslovakia. They have a muscular, rectangular body, short legs and dropped medium-sized ears. They also have medium-sized eyes in brown, dark brown or reddish-brown colors and a long head. Their long, silky with slight curls coat comes in shades of gray or rarely, brown. They are also longer than they are tall. Moreover, Cesky Terriers have a calm and kind expression. They are also less active and quieter compared to other terriers.

# Chihuahua

Chihuahua is the smallest breed of dog. They come in a wide variety of head shapes, colors, and coat lengths. They may have heads shaped like an apple or head shaped like a deer's head. They may also have long coat as well as short coat. When it comes to colors, they may come in black, white, chestnut, fawn, sand, silver, sable, steel blue, or black & tan. A Chihuahua's body is longer than it is tall. Furthermore, they have a large, round eyes in dark, ruby, and or lighter colors, large, upright ears and long tail. They are also easily provoked to attack but loyal to one particular person. They love their dens and will often burrow themselves in pillows, clothes hampers, and blankets.

# Chow Chow

Chow Chows or simple Chows are ancient dogs from northern China, where they are referred to as *Songshi Quan*, meaning "puffy-lion dog". They have also been called the *Tang Quan*, "Dog of the Tang Empire." They have a muscular body, broad skull, small, triangular ears, almond-shaped eyes, and straight hind legs. Additionally, they have a blue-black/purple tongue, blue lips, black or blue nose and curly tail. They also have a thick coat, especially in their neck area. Their coat may be in red, black, blue, cinnamon, or cream colors. It is also Chow Chows nature to be protective, quiet and well behaved, and resistant to training.

# Dachshund

Dachshunds are short-legged and long-bodied dogs. They were developed to smell, chase, and flush out badgers and other burrow-dwelling animals. Their long body is muscular while their short legs are stout. Their front paws are also unusually large for digging purposes. They also have a long snout and short or long or wired hair in different colors including: black, red, chocolate, tan, cream and blue or any combination of those colors. Furthermore, Dachshunds have dark red or brown-black almond-shaped eyes, long dropped ears, and medium length tail. They are also noted as playful, but stubborn dogs who love to chase small animals, birds and tennis balls.

# Dalmatian

Dalmatians are large dogs with unique black or reddish-brown spotted coat. Most of their spots are on their head or ears. These days, they are popular family pets. Their length and height is proportion. They have a muscular body, round feet, dark-colored nose, thin ears and eyes in brown, amber, or blue colors. However, some dogs have one blue eye and one brown eye, or other combinations. Aside from their usual white and black/reddish-brown color, on rare occasions, Dalmatians may also have blue, orange or lemon colors and brindle, mosaic or tricolored coat patterns. Dalmatian puppies are born with plain white coats. Their spots will begin to appear within 3 to 4 weeks after birth. Dalmatians are also playful, happy, easy going and very dedicated dogs

# Dandie Dinmont Terrier

Dandie Dinmont Terriers are small dogs with long body, short legs, and a distinctive hair on top of their head. They also have a dark-colored nose and silky, thick coat in either "pepper" or "mustard" colors. Their pepper color ranges from a dark bluish black to a very light silvery gray. On the other hand, mustard color varies from reddish brown to a fawn where the head appears to be almost white. Usually, their legs and feet are of a darker color than their body. Dandie Dinmont Terriers are generally tough, but usually friendly, and are suitable for older children. They usually are excellent companion and guard dogs.

# Doberman Pinscher

Doberman Pinschers are also known as Dobermann, or Doberman. They are medium-large dogs from Germany. They have a square muscular build, a nose in either black, dark brown, dark gray, dark tan or pink colors, a long head and a short, thick coat in a variety of colors including: black, black with tan markings, blue-gray, red, fawn and white. They also have upright ears, broad chest, straight legs and almond-shaped eyes in various shades of brown. Doberman Pinschers have a proud, watchful, determined, and obedient temperament.

# English Cocker Spaniel

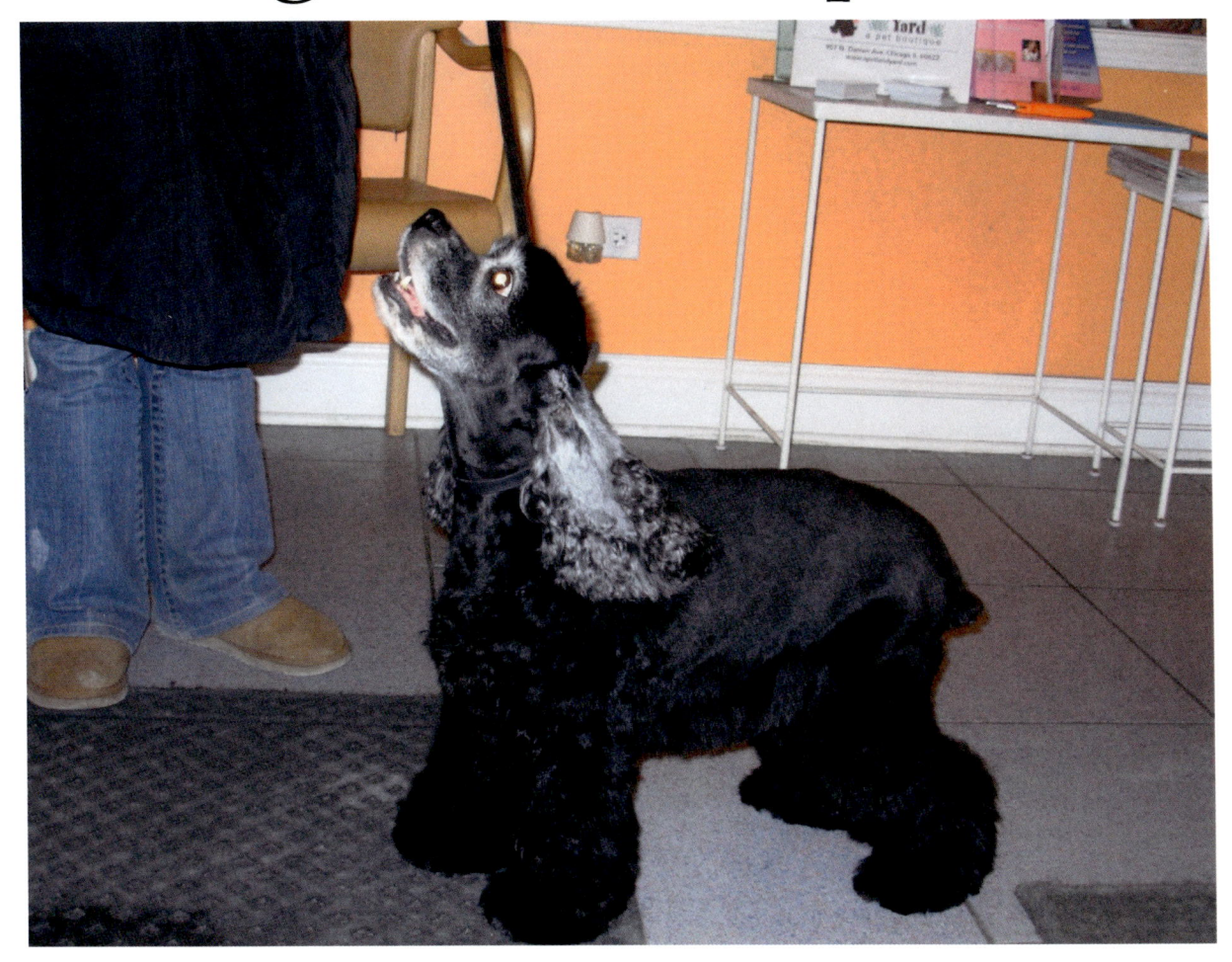

English Cocker Spaniels are active, good-natured dogs noted for their intelligence and alertness. They have oval, dark brown or hazel eyes, long ears, long muzzle (nose and mouth part), and black or brown nose. Additionally, they have straight legs, cat-like feet, and medium length hair in black, reddish-brown, red or combination of white with black and reddish-brown or red markings. English Cocker Spaniels have two varieties: field and show. The show types have longer coats than the field/working types. Show types are those that are entered in a dog show (competition for dog appearance). Working dogs, on the other hand, are those that perform tasks to assist humans.

# English Setter

English Setters are medium-sized dogs with an elegant overall appearance. They were developed to hunt quail, pheasant, and grouse. They have a slightly domed head, dark eyes, folded ears, and length proportionate to their height. Furthermore, they have a long tail, short to medium coat and additional long silky coat or "feathering" outside their ears, neck, chest, on their tail, under their belly and on their legs. Show type English Setters have long, flowing coat that requires regular grooming. However, field or hunting type English Setters have shorter coat that requires less grooming. The color of their coat is white with colored speckles that come in many colors like black, orange or reddish brown. English Setters are also energetic, people-oriented, and are very-well suited to families.

# English Springer Spaniel

English Springer Spaniels are well-proportioned dogs traditionally used for helping hunters. They are medium in size and have moderately long featherings on their legs and tail. They also have a reddish-brown or black nose, long ears, oval and medium-sized eyes in either dark hazel or dark brown, and straight front legs. Their coat is of medium-length and with feathering on legs, ears, and cheeks. Their coat also comes in different color combinations such as, white with black or reddish-brown markings. English Springers are even-tempered, gentle, friendly, and sociable dogs that make great child companions. They are also intelligent, skillful, willing and obedient.

# Field Spaniel

Field Spaniels are medium-sized dogs. They have long, dark, silky coat in black, reddish-brown or roan colors with tan points or white markings on their throat. They also have longer fur on their chest, belly, ears and on the back of their legs. They have large nose in light brown, dark brown or black, medium-sized almond-shaped eyes in dark hazel to brown colors and medium-length ears. Field Spaniels are also active, independent, easygoing, charming, affectionate, intelligent and playful.

# Finnish Spitz

Finnish Spitz is a dog from Finland. They were originally used to hunt different animals like squirrels, rodents or bears. In appearance, they resemble a fox. They have a muscular, square body, black nose and lips and dark, almond-shaped eyes. Finnish Spitz also has upright ears, straight legs, deep chest, curled tail and round, cat-like feet. Their straight, harsh coat comes in various shades of golden-red, red-brown, yellowish-red and honey-colored, with or without small white markings. Additionally, Finnish Spitz is friendly, active, playful, keen and can be trained, if the owner has a natural, gentle, calm, authority to them.

# French Bulldog

French Bulldogs are small domestic dogs. They have a stocky little body, large square head, black nose, and upper lips that hang down over their lower lips. They also have dark round eyes, upright bat-like ears, straight or corkscrew tail and skin that form wrinkles around their head and shoulders. French Bulldogs have short coat in different colors including: brindle (tiger-striped), brindle and white, cream, cream and white, fawn, fawn and white, white, white and fawn, black, black and fawn, black and white, etc. Usually, they have black markings on their face. When it comes to their behavior, French Bulldogs are pleasant, playful, alert, affectionate, enthusiastic and lively.

# German Pinscher

German Pinschers are medium-sized dogs from Germany. They are also called as Standard Pinschers. They have black nose and lips, medium-sized oval eyes, folded or upright ears and strong, smooth, glossy coat in colors like red fawn, black and tan, and dark brown with yellow markings. However, black with tan markings are the most common. German Pinschers are ideal companion dogs that are brave, have considerable stamina, lively and a vocal guard dog.

# German Shepherd Dog

German Shepherds or German Shepherd Dogs are medium to large-sized working dogs from Germany. They were developed originally for herding sheep. However, due to their strength, intelligence, trainability, and obedience, they have been used for disability assistance, search-and-rescue, police and military roles and acting. They are also considered as the second-most popular breed of dog in the United States. They are well proportioned dogs with muscular body, black nose, dark almond-shaped eyes, erect ears, bushy tail and strong legs. Their long coat comes in black with tan or all black. Often used as working dogs, German Shepherds are courageous, keen, alert and fearless. They are also cheerful, obedient and eager to learn.

# Giant Schnauzer

Giant Schnauzers are working dogs from Germay. They were originally developed to assist in farms by driving livestock to market and guarding the farmer's property. They were also used to guard breweries, butchers' shops, stockyards and factories. They have a thick coat that protects them from the weather. Their coat also comes in two color pattern: solid black and pepper and salt. Pepper and salt is alternating white and black that makes their coat appear gray at a distance. They also have a distinct beard, eyebrows, rectangular head, large black nose, black lips and dark oval eyes. They are also intelligent and loyal dogs which are now used as police dogs.

# Golden Retriever

Golden Retrievers are sturdy, medium to large sized dogs. They have a broad skull, black or brownish black nose, dark brown eyes, short drooping ears and a thick tail. Their water-resistant coat is thick and comes in cream to a rich golden color. Golden Retrievers are also lovable, well-mannered, intelligent and always patient and gentle with children, making them popular as family dogs.

# Great Dane

Great Danes are large German dogs especially known for their giant size. They are one of the tallest dog breeds in the world. In fact, the world record holder for the tallest dog was a Great Dane called Zeus (died September 2014; aged 5), who measured 44 inches from paw to shoulder. They are powerful dogs with square body, long rectangular head, black or blue nose, and dark medium-sized eyes. Their front legs are perfectly straight and their short coat comes in brindle, fawn, black, blue and merle (or patched pattern) colors. Great Danes are often called as "gentle giant" because of their charming and affectionate personality. They are also playful and patient with children.

# Greater Swiss Mountain Dog

Greater Swiss Mountain Dogs are dogs which were developed in the Swiss Alps in Switzerland. They are large dogs with great physical strength and agility. Their coat color usually comes in black base with specific rust and white markings. Their rust markings appear in a spot over each eye, on the cheeks and on either side of the chest. However, their white appears as a blaze on their snout, chest, and on the tip of their tail. There may also have white collar or patches of white on their neck. Furthermore, Greater Swiss Mountain Dogs have black nose and lips, almond-shaped eyes in hazel to chestnut colors, triangular ears, and straight front legs. Greater Swiss Mountain Dogs are also sociable, active, calm, and loves being part of the family.

# Greenland Dog

Greenland Dogs are also known as Greenland Husky. They are large dogs kept as sled dogs and for hunting polar bear and seal. Sled dogs are dogs used to pull a sleigh. They have a thick stand-off outer coat and a thick undercoat that allows them to withstand living in temperatures that can reach -50 to -75 degrees Fahrenheit. Their coat also comes in many color or color combination of black, white, cream, chocolate, tan, blue, red and light brown. They also have small triangular ears, broad head, extremely powerful jaws and a large, bushy tail, which is curled over their back. The legs are also well feathered and the toes are thickly furred with large pads. Typically, Greenland Dogs are aloof and very independent, but are loving as well with an owner he bonds with.

# Havanese

Havanese is the national dog of Cuba. They are also referred to as "Havana Silk Dogs", They are small in size with strong body and a tail which is carried over to their back. They also have dropped and folded ears and dark eyes. Their long and silky coat comes in all colors including: cream, gold, white, silver, blue and black. Havanese is an ideal family pet and a true companion dog because of their highly adaptable and social personality.

# Ibizan Hound

Ibizan Hounds are hunting dogs also called as Podenco Ibicenco. They have two hair types: the more common smooth type and the wire type. They also have a slender body, long and narrow head, a rosy flesh colored nose and small eyes in clear amber to caramel in color. Additionally, Ibizan Hounds have large, erect ears, long neck, straight front legs and coat in colors like white and red, white and tan, solid white or solid red. They are also regarded as quiet, playful and polite dogs that are good with children, gentle, sensible and sensitive.

# Irish Wolfhound

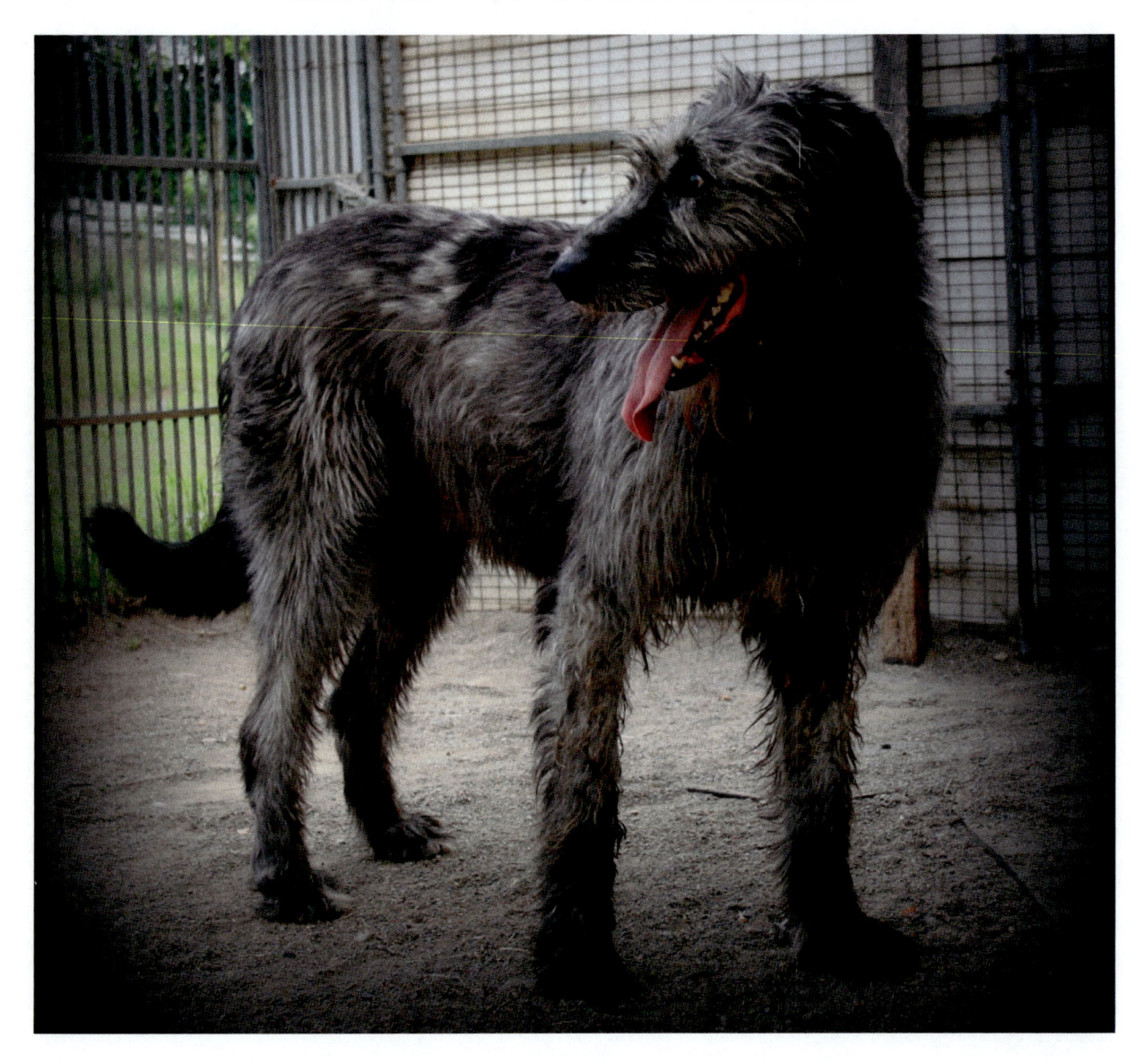

Irish Wolfhounds are domestic dogs from Ireland. Their name was derived from their purpose—wolf hunting with dogs. They are giant-sized dogs, probably, one of the tallest in the world, reaching the size of a small pony. They have a long head, small ears, long neck and long tail. Their legs are also long and strong with round feet. The wiry, shaggy coat is longer over the eyes and under the jaw and comes in gray, brindle, red, black, pure white or fawn colors. Gray Irish Wolfhounds, however, are the most common. Furthermore, they are also sweet-tempered, patient, kind, thoughtful and very intelligent. Their excellent nature can be trusted with children.

# Italian Greyhound

Italian Greyhounds are small dogs, sometimes called an "I.G." or an "Iggy". They have a slender body, long head, black or brown nose, and medium-sized dark eyes. Moreover, they have long neck, straight front legs and thin tail. Their short, glossy coat comes in all colors like gray, slate gray, red, fawn, blue, black, white or cream. They can also be white with color markings or color with white markings on the chest and feet. When it comes to their behavior, Italian Greyhounds are playful, keen, affectionate, intelligent and kind-mannered. They are generally submissive and want nothing more than to please their owner.

# Jack Russell Terrier

Jack Russell Terriers are small terriers with well-proportioned body (length in proportion to the height). They also have a proportioned head, black nose, dark almond shaped eyes, strong legs with round feet and smooth coat. The color of their coat is: predominantly white with tan, black or brown markings. Jack Russell Terriers are also known for being cheerful, merry, devoted and loving dogs. It is also in their nature to be spirited, obedient and fearless. They also enjoy games and playing with toys.

# Japanese Chin

Japanese Chins, also known as Japanese Spaniels are known for Strabismus on their large protruding eyes. Strabismus is a condition where the eyes do not properly align with each other. It prevents them from directing both eyes simultaneously towards the same point. They also have small, V-shaped ears that hang down, wide, black nose, and strong legs. Their coat comes in white with colored patches which are often black, but can also be red, lemon, orange or sable. Japanese Chins may also be in black and white with tan points or brindle (tiger-striped). Obviously, they are charming dogs with lively, and happy personality. They are also pleasant, loving, intelligent, affectionate and extremely devoted to their master.

# Japanese Spitz

Japanese Spitz is a small to medium dog which serves as a companion dog and pet. Their long coat is always pure white in color. Their tail is covered with long hair and is carried curled over their back. Their ears are also small, pointed and upright. They also have large oval and slightly slanted eyes in dark color, black nose and lips and legs with long hair. Japanese Spitz is typically high-spirited, intelligent and playful dog, which is alert and obedient. It is also good watchdog and will alert its owners when it feels it is necessary.

# Karelian Bear Dog

Karelian Bear Dogs (KBD) is regarded as a national treasure in Finland. They hunt a variety of animals including bears, moose, and wild boar. They have small ears, small eyes, thighs covered in thick hair, and a distinctive black and white coat. However, copper tinted Karelian Bear Dogs also appear. Their distinct white markings occur on their head, neck, chest, abdomen and legs. Their jaws are also powerful and the tail is long. Moreover, they have curled tail and well-proportioned body. They are also sensitive, independent, intelligent, skillful, and energetic.

# Keeshond

Keeshond is a medium-sized dog from Germany and is called the German Spitz, more specifically the Wolfspitz. They have a long, straight coat in silver and black, a curled tail carried over their back, dark eyes, and erect, triangular ears. They also have catlike rounded feet. Keeshond is also an excellent children's companion that is active, intelligent, very keen and outgoing. It can also be trained to perform

# Komondor

Komondor is also known as the Hungarian Sheepdog. They are large, white-colored dogs used to guard livestock. They are also sometimes referred to as 'mop dogs,' due to their long, corded coat. They are powerful dogs with massive bone structure, large head and dark brown almond-shaped eyes. They also have elongated ears and long tail. Komondor can be a good family dog if they have an owner who knows how to display a natural, firm authority over the dog and are raised with children from the start.

# Kuvasz

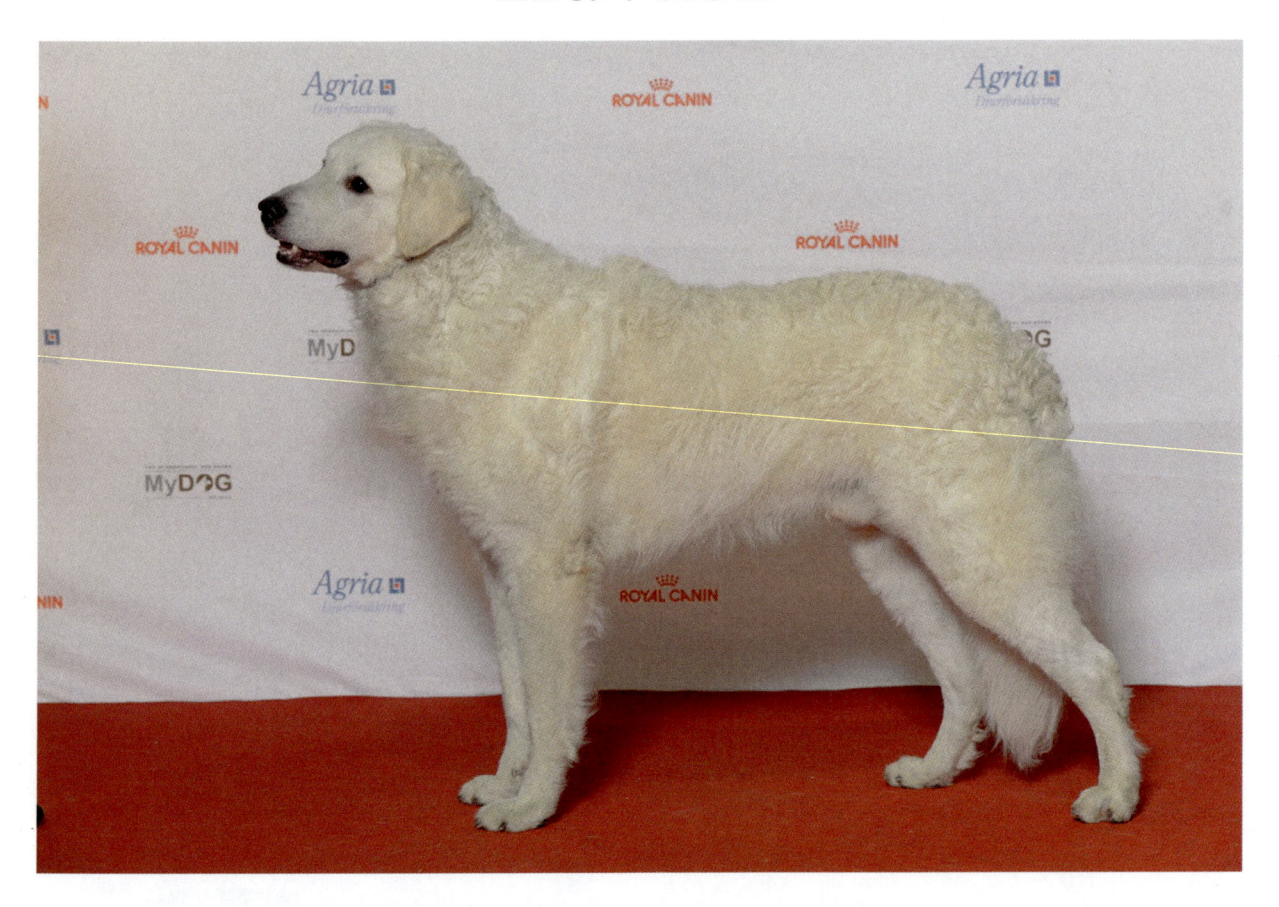

Kuvasz is an ancient dog from Hungary, where it was historically been used as a royal guard dog, or to guard livestock. They are fearless dogs with their head considered the most beautiful part of their body. They have a black nose and lips, V-shaped and slightly rounded ears, dark brown almond-shaped eyes and a strong body. Their hair is shorter on their feet and head. However, on their body and legs, their wavy hair can be as much as 4-6 inches long. Their coat comes in white and ivory colors only. Kuvasz is also an intelligent dog, very territorial and has a strong protective instinct.

# Labrador Retriever

Labrador Retrievers or Labradors are hunting dogs and are one of the most popular breeds of dog in the United Kingdom and the United States. There are two types of Labradors, the English Labrador and the American Labrador. The English bred Lab comes from English bred stock with general appearance different from the American bred Lab. The English bred Lab is heavier, thicker and blockier. The American bred Lab on the other hand comes from American bred stock and is tall and lanky. Their smooth water-resistant coat has colors ranging from solid black to yellow or to chocolate. Both types have a broad head, black or brown nose, and medium-sized eyes in hazel, brown, green or greenish-yellow or gray colors. They also have webbed feet that helps them in swimming. Labrador Retrievers are loyal, loving, affectionate and patient, making a great family dog.

# Lhasa Apso

Lhasa Apsos are dogs from Tibet. They were bred to alert the monks in Buddhist Monasteries to any intruders who entered. Their name Lhasa Apso simply means "long-haired Lhasa (Tibetan) dog". They are small dogs with small, dark brown eyes, thick-haired ears, straight front legs and round and catlike feet. Their thick coat is straight and long over their entire body, reaching to the floor. They coat also comes in any color, however, gold, cream and honey are the most popular. Owners often cut the dogs' hair short to make them easier to care for. They also make a good pet due to their friendly, intelligent, lively and assertive manner.

# Maltese

Maltese dogs are small dogs from the Central Mediterranean Area. They have a small body, slightly rounded skull, heavily feathered ears, large black eyes, and black nose. They also have a long and silky coat that is white or light ivory in color. A lot of owners choose to cut the coat short for easy-care. Maltese dogs are spirited, lively and playful. They are also gentle, loving, trusting and devoted to their master. Additionally, they are highly intelligent dogs that are good at learning tricks, bold and quick to sound the alarm in case of suspicious noises.

# Norwich Terrier

Norwich Terriers are dogs from the United Kingdom. They were bred to hunt small vermin (pests) or rodents. They are also one of the smallest terriers that are relatively rare. Norwich Terriers are strong, little dogs that have a wide head, small and oval shaped dark eyes, medium sized upright ears and straight legs with round feet. They also have a wiry, straight coat (about 1 ½ to 2 inches long. Their coats come in many colors including: red, wheaten, tan, black and tan, or grizzle with or without dark points and white markings. Typically, they are friendly, active, courageous, and affectionate.

# Otterhound

Otterhounds are dogs with no known origins. They have a slightly rectangular body, large head, large dark nose, dark or hazel eyes and long ears. They also have webbed feet with arched toes. Their rough, course and water resistant coat comes in all hound colors including but not limited to grizzle or wheaten with black markings. Otterhounds also have a shaggy face and bushy eyebrows. Their behavior is fearless, devoted to its family, good with children, friendly, loving and happy with a lot of spirit.

# Papillon

Papillons are also called the Continental Toy Spaniel. They derived their name from the butterfly-like look of their long and fringed hair on the ears. They have a small head, dark, medium-sized, round eyes, large ears, and a long tail covered with fine hair. They also have extra hair on their chest, ears, back of the legs and the tail. Their coat color is white with patches of any color. A mask of a color other than white covers both ears and eyes from back to front. The temperament of a Papillon is a happy, friendly and adventurous. They are excellent family dogs but should be watched around little children.

# Pekingese

Pekingese dogs are also known as the Lion Dog, Peking Lion Dog, Pelchie Dog, or Peke. They are ancient dogs from China where they are favored by the royalty of the Chinese Imperial court, Chinese Buddhist Monks and are owned by Chinese princes. Pekingese is a small, well-balanced, dog. It has a muscular body that is slightly longer than it is tall. Its head is large with flat front face, black nose, large, prominent, round eyes and heart-shaped feathered ears. It also has a short neck, short and thick legs, and long and coarse coat that come in all colors, sometimes with a black mask or black markings on the face. Pekingese is a very brave little dog, sensitive, independent and extremely affectionate with its master and can make wonderful companion. If overfed, the Pekingese will quickly become overweight.

# Pomeranian

Pomeranians, also known as a Pom or Pom Pom are dogs that have been made popular by a number of royal owners since the 18th century. Queen Victoria owned a particularly small Pomeranian. Pomeranians are small, toy-sized dog. They have dark almond-shaped eyes, small, erect ears, feathered tail and a thick coat that is longer around the neck and chest area. They come in a variety of coat colors and patterns including red, orange, white, cream, blue, brown, black, black and tan, wolf sable, orange sable, brindle and parti-color, which is white with colored markings. Pomeranians are also a proud, lively little dog that are intelligent, eager to learn and very loyal to their handler and family. They are a wonderful companion and show dog.

# Poodle

Poodles are dogs originally bred in Germany. They have a moderately rounded skull, dark, oval-shaped eyes in black or brown, long ears that hang close to their head and legs that are proportion with their size. Their coat is either curly or corded and comes in all solid colors including black, blue, silver, gray, cream, apricot, red, white, or brown. Poodles are remarkably intelligent, highly responsive and referred to as one of the most trainable breeds. They are also sweet, cheerful, lively and like to be with people.

# Pug

Pugs are dogs with wrinkly, short muzzle (nose and mouth area) and curled tail. In the nineteenth century Queen Victoria developed a passion for Pugs which she passed on to other members of the Royal family. They have a short coat that is soft, fine and smooth and comes in apricot, fawn, black and silver colors. However, the most common are black and fawn. Pugs also have a small but well-developed body muscles, round head, moles on the cheeks, very large, dark eyes and small, thin ears. Additionally, Pugs are keen, happy-go-lucky, spirited, loyal, loving and affectionate with their family.

# Puli

Puli is a small to medium dog from Hungary where it was used to herd and guard livestock animals. It is best known for its long, corded coat that is waterproof and comes in colors like black, any shade of gray, apricot (with or without a black mask) and the rarer white. It resembles a Komondor. However, Komondor is much larger than the Puli. Furthermore, Puli also has a muscular body, curled tail, almond-shaped and dark brown eyes and medium-sized ears. A full adult coat can reach to the ground. The Puli is a lively, cheerful little dog that is very loyal and an excellent family pet.

# Pumi

Pumi is a small dog from Hungary. It has an elongated muzzle, slightly oblique and dark eyes, a tail that is always carried high, upright ears, and hind feet that are set back from the body. Its medium-length, curled coat comes in colors like black, all shades of gray and reddish brown. Pumi is a multi-functional dog. It is a strong sheepdog, but also a successful guard dog and hunting dog.

# Pyrenean Mastiff

Pyrenean Mastiffs are large dogs from the Aragonese Pyrenees in Spain. They are very large where males reach 77 cm in height and females 71 cm. They can also be up to 81 cm in height. They have a massive, broad head, a thick skull and strong bones. They also have a long, fringed tail, sparkly dark eyes, a black nose and pointed ears. Their thick, weather-resistant, medium-length coat grows longer on their throat and neck. Their coat is white with dark spots and a well-defined mask or face markings in deep gold, dusk, black, light tan, sand, brindle, red or any shade of gray. Pyrenean Mastiffs are self-reliant, calm, and is protective with children. They are also gentle with other dogs as well as other pets and people it knows. However, if provoked, they will not hesitate to defend their family or itself from a perceived threat.

# Rhodesian Ridgeback

Rhodesian Ridgebacks are dogs from Zimbabwe. They are also previously known as Van Rooyen's Lion Dog, African Lion Hound or African Lion Dog because of their ability to keep a lion at bay while awaiting its master's arrival to make the hunt. Rhodesian Ridgebacks are large dogs with broad head, black, brown or reddish-brown nose, a black tongue and round (usually) brown eyes. Moreover, they also have medium-sized ears, very straight and strong front legs and a fairly long tail. Their coat is short and thick with a clearly defined ridge of hairs that grows in opposite direction down the middle of their back. Their coat colors include light wheaten (brown) to shades of red sometimes with a little white on the chest and toes. As a hunter, they are ferocious in the hunt, but at home, they are calm, gentle, obedient and good dogs.

# Rottweiler

Rottweilers large dogs which were used to herd livestock and pull carts with butchered meat to market. Today, they are being used as search and rescue dogs, as guide dogs for the blind, as guard dogs and police dogs. Rottweilers have a muscular and powerful body, wide black nose, black lips and almond shaped eyes in dark color. Furthermore, Rottweilers also have triangular ears, broad chest and short, hard and thick coat in black with rust to mahogany markings on the cheeks, muzzle, paws and legs. However, a red colored Rottweiler with brown markings also exists. Rottweilers are powerful, calm, trainable, loyal, protective and courageous dogs that are devoted to their owner and family.

# Saluki

Salukis are dogs classed as sighthounds or dogs that hunt by sight. They typically have long legs, slim body, long head, black or reddish-brown nose and large, oval eyes in dark to hazel colors. They also have long ears, long neck and feet that are thickly haired between the toes for protection. . Their coat is short with long, silky feathering on the ears and tail and is in a wide variety of colors including: white, cream, fawn, golden, red, grizzle and tan, black and white and black and tan. The Salukis are also noted for being gentle, friendly, even-tempered and extremely devoted. However, they can be somewhat aloof, even with their family.

# Samoyed

The Samoyed is a dog that takes its name from the Samoyedic peoples (people that speak Samoyedic) of Siberia. They help with the herding, and to pull sleds when they moved. They have a muscular body, black, brown or reddish-brown nose, black lips and dark, almond-shaped eyes. They also have erect, triangular ears, moderately long tail that is well-covered with hair and muscular legs. Their thick and straight coat has colors including pure white, yellow and cream. The Samoyed is a gentle dog which is very devoted, easygoing, friendly and quite playful. They also love everyone and will gladly be friendly to all, including intruders.

# Scottish Deerhound

Scottish Deerhounds, or simply Deerhounds are large dogs once used to hunt the Red Deer. They are tall and slim dogs with a nose in black or blue colors, eyes that are either brown or hazel, folded ears, and straight front legs. Their coat is longer on their body, neck, beard, mustache and mane, and is shorter on their head, chest and belly. The coat color includes shades of blue gray, gray, brindle and black, yellow and sandy red or red fawn. Scottish Deerhounds are gentle, well-mannered dog, polite, affectionate, loving, friendly and excellent with children.

# Shar Pei

Shar Peis or Chinese Shar-Peis are dogs known for their distinctive wrinkles and blue-black tongue. Their name was derived from a British word which means "sand skin" and refers to the texture of their short, rough coat. As puppies, Shar Pei have numerous wrinkles. As they mature, these wrinkles loosen and spread out as they "grow into their skin". In 1978, they were considered as one of the world's rarest dog breeds by *TIME* magazine and the *Guinness World Records*. Additionally, they have almond-shaped eyes, triangular ears and coat colors including all solid colors and sables (dark chocolate brown). They are also very loyal to their handler, intelligent playful, active, dominant, and brave. They bond with their family and are friendly toward strangers.

# Shih Tzu

Shih Tzus are also known as Chrysanthemum Dogs. Their exact origins are unknown. However, it is thought to have originated in Tibet and then have been developed in China. They are small dogs with a body that is slightly longer than it is tall. They also have a round head, broad nose, large and round eyes and large dropped ears. Their thick and long coat comes in all colors. The hair above their eyes is often tied in a topknot. They also have a beard and mustache. Shih Tzus are alert, lively, little dog. They are also gentle, loyal, make friends easily and respond well to consistent, patient training.

# Siberian Husky

Siberian Huskies are medium-sized dogs from north-eastern Siberia. They are recognizable by their thick fur, erect triangular ears, and distinctive markings (white facial mask or markings and white legs and underside). They are strong dogs used to pull a sled. They have a medium-sized head, black, tan or flesh colored nose, oval-shaped eyes that come in blue, brown, amber or any combination thereof and a tail that is carried over their back. Their medium-length coat is thick and can withstand temperatures as low as -58° to -76° F (-50° to -60° C). Their coat colors include all, from black to pure white, with or without markings on the head. Their face mask and underside are usually white, and the remaining coat any color. Some of the common colors are black and white, red and white, brown, gray and white, silver, wolf-gray and sable and white. Siberian Huskies are loving, gentle, playful, happy-go-lucky dogs that are fond of their families.

# Silken Windhound

Silken Windhounds are rare American dogs with exceptional running ability. They are small and elegant sighthounds or dogs that hunt by sight. They have an athletic build and luxurious, silky coat that comes in any combination of coat colors and markings, from spotted to solid, black and tan, saddled, brindle and sable, pure white and reds to deep black and blues, and a rainbow of colors in between. They also have a long arched neck, long tail covered with long hair, and a beautiful curved body. More long hairs are present on their face and on the back of their legs. Silken Windhounds are intelligent and responsive hound that demonstrates a strong desire to please their human companions.

# St. Bernard

St. Bernards are very large dogs from Swiss Alps, north Italy and Switzerland. They were originally bred for rescue purposes. They have become famous through tales of alpine rescues, as well as for their enormous size. They have a strong, muscular body, a massive head, a broad nose and black lips. They also have dark medium-sized eyes, dropped ears, muscular legs and a long tail. St. Bernards have two types of coat: rough and smooth, which are both very thick and come in white with markings in tan, red, mahogany, brindle and black, all in various combinations. Their face and ears are also usually black. Rough-coated dogs have slightly longer hair especially on their thighs and legs. When it comes to their personality, they are extremely gentle, friendly and very tolerant of children. They are also slow moving, patient, obedient, extremely loyal, eager and willing to please.

# Standard Schnauzer

Standard Schnauzers are dogs from Germany. The literal translation for the German word Schnauzer is "snouter" or "moustache", because of the dog's distinctively bearded snout. They are medium-sized dog with large nose, black lips, oval-shaped eyes that are dark brown in color, upright or dropped ears and small feet with black nails. Aside from a beard, they also have a moustache and eyebrows. Their coat is thick and hard with color ranging from solid black and salt and pepper (alternating black and white that gives a gray appearance). Standard Schnauzers are great watch and guard dog. They are also lively, but not restless if provided with enough exercise, enthusiastic, spunky and affectionate,

# Tibetan Spaniel

Tibetan Spaniels are assertive, small and intelligent dogs originating over 2,500 years ago in the Himalayan mountains of Tibet. They are often mistaken for the Pekingese, the differences being that the Tibetan Spaniel has a less profuse coat, slightly longer face and does not have the extra skin around their eyes. Their body is also somewhat longer than tall. They have a small head, black nose, dark brown eyes and hare-like feet. Their tail is also covered with hair and carried over their back. Tibetan Spaniels have silky coat especially on the neck which comes in all colors, solid, multi-colored or shaded, including fawn, red, gold, cream, white, black and black and tan, often with white markings on the feet. Tibetan Spaniels are as well cheerful, happy, charming, very clever and trusting.

# Toy Fox Terrier

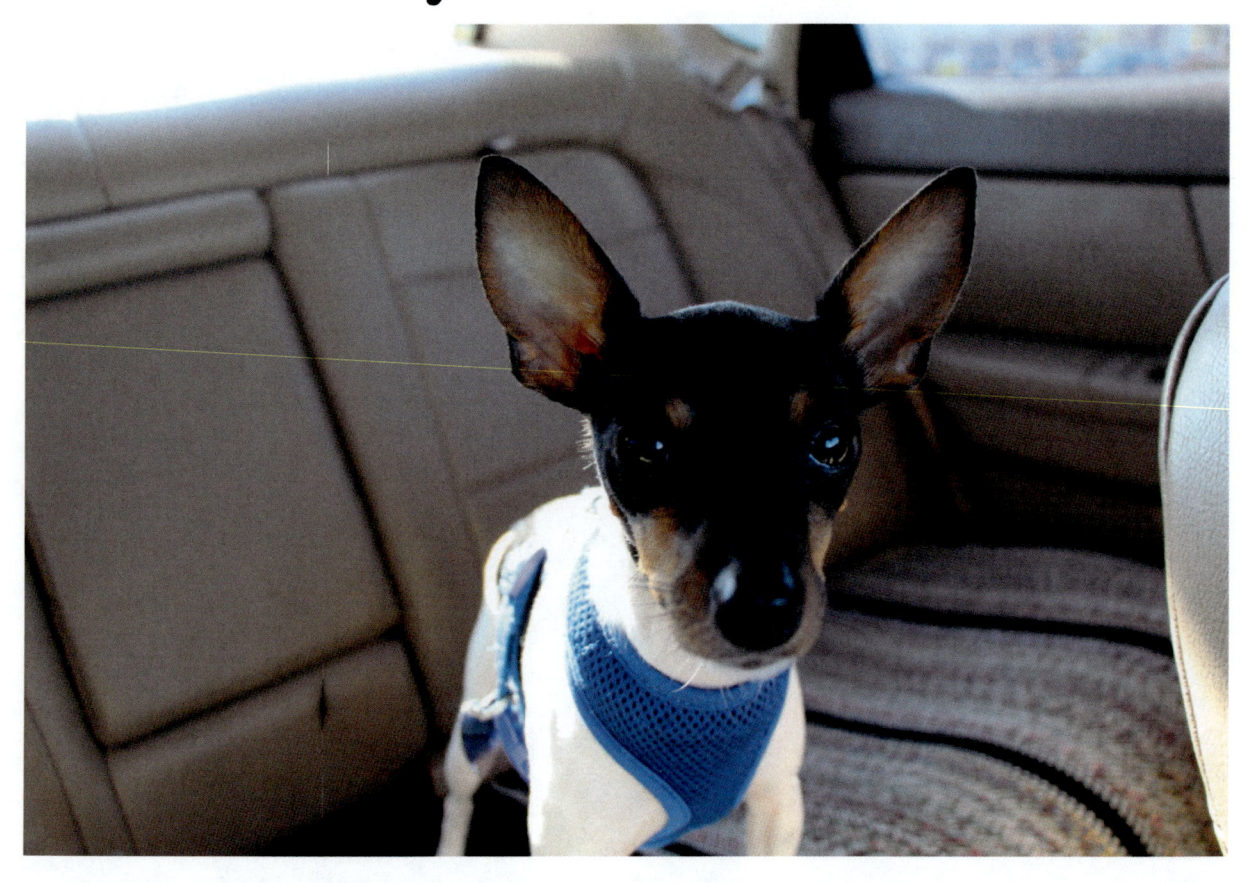

Toy Fox Terrier s are small dogs also known as the American Toy Terrier or Amertoy. They have a black or chocolate nose, dark and round eyes, V-shaped ears and short tail. Their short coat is tricolor, predominately white with black and tan markings. The breed is also typically tough and bright, and can be stubborn without proper leadership from his owners. They are also curious, active, intelligent, loving, sensitive and pleasant.

# Welsh Terrier

Welsh Terriers are dogs from Wales and were originally bred for hunting fox, rodents and badger. However, during the last century, they have been mainly used for dog show competitions. They have a rectangular head, small dark brown eyes, V-shaped ears and small cat-like feet. Their coat is hard and thick with bushy eyebrows, mustache and beard. Colors include black and tan and grizzle with a black jacket marking over the back. Puppies are born all black and as their coats lighten the jacket marking remains black. Welsh Terriers are vigilant, active, cheerful dogs that are affectionate, intelligent, loving, devoted, playful and happy.

# West Highland White Terrier

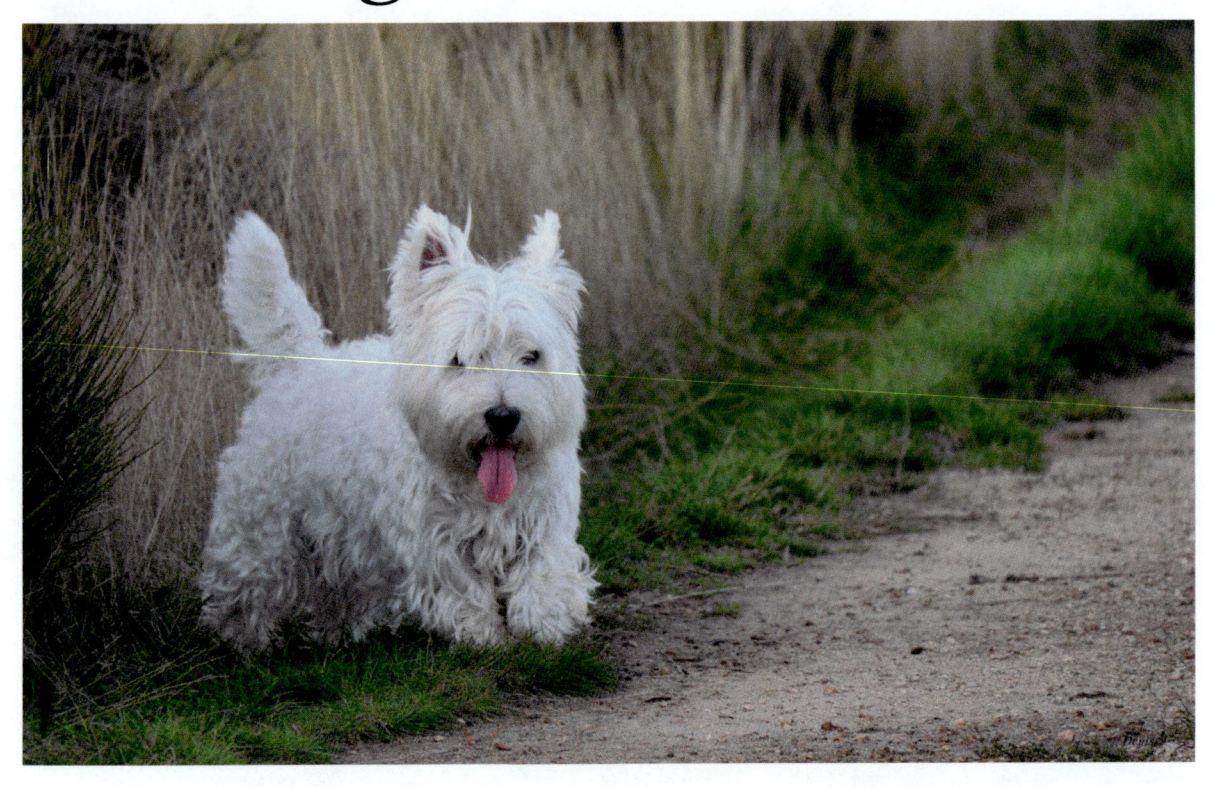

West Highland White Terriers are commonly known as the Westie or Westy. They are Scottish dogs with a distinctive white coat. They have a head that is in proportion to their size, black nose, dark brown eyes, triangular ears and short legs. They also have a short tail and coat that is about 2 inches long and comes in solid white. West Highland White Terriers are easy to train, fairly friendly toward strangers and gets along well with children.

# Whippet

Whippets or English Whippets or Snap Dogs are medium-sized dogs from England. They have also been described as "the poor man's racehorse" because they have been used in dog racings. They have a long skull, a nose in black, dark blue or dark brown color, small ears, and dark oval-shaped eyes. They also have a long tail and short, smooth coat that comes in all colors including brindle, black, red, fawn, tiger white or slate blue, either solid-colored or mixed. Whippets are intelligent, lively, affectionate, sweet and docile. They are also very devoted companion, quiet and calm in the home.

# White Shepherd

White Shepherds are similar to and looks the same as the German Shepherds except for their coat color. They also often have longer fur than the traditional German Shepherd Dogs. Furthermore, White Shepherds have an overall more square and upright look and lighter frame as compared to German Shepherd Dogs. The stiff and long coat of White Shepherds is also always white in color. Additionally, they are courageous, keen, alert and fearless. They are also cheerful, obedient, eager to learn, confident, serious and clever. White Shepherds are extremely faithful and brave.

# Wirehaired Vizsla

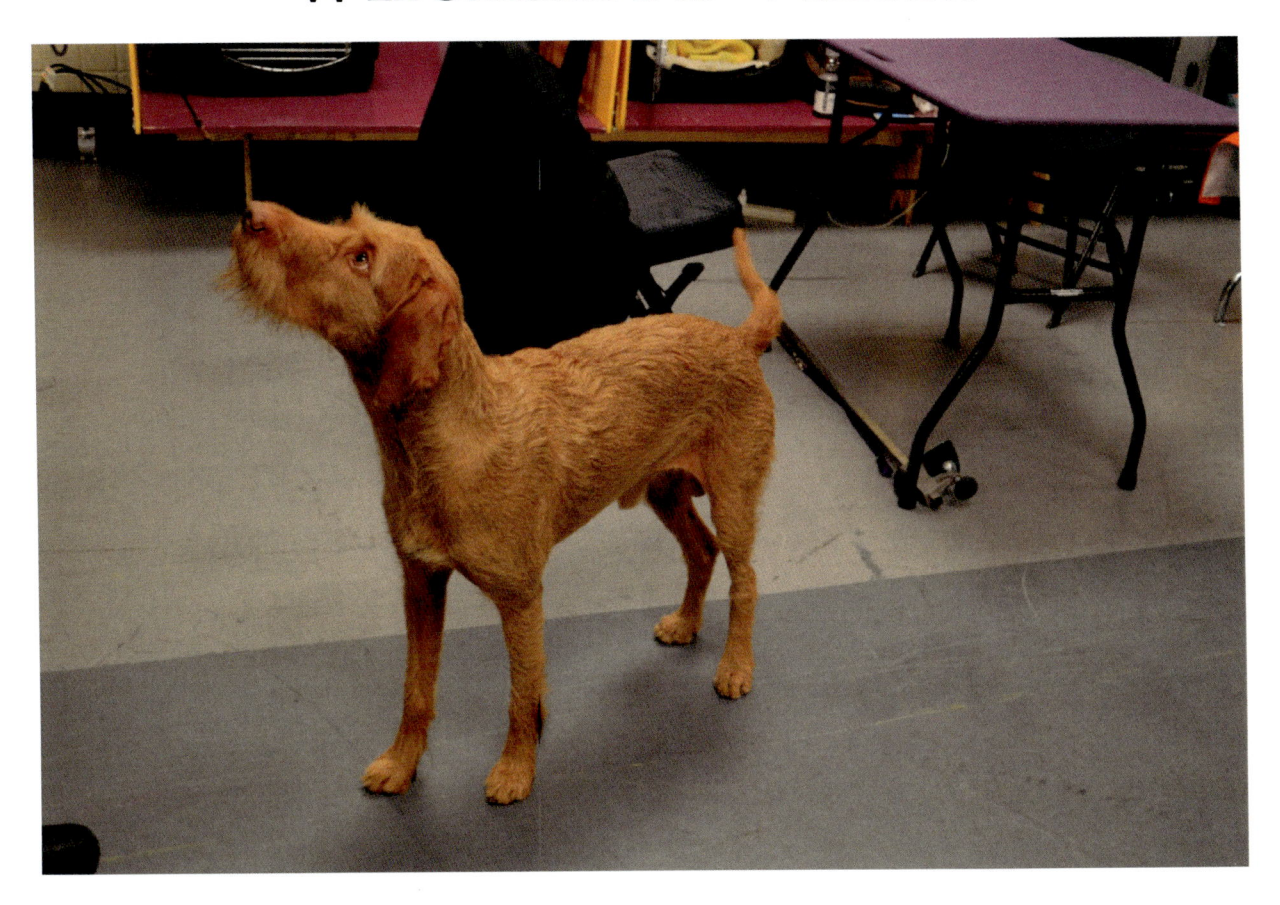

Wirehaired Vizslas are dogs from Hungary. They are known as excellent hunting dogs. They have an excellent nose, lean head, strong jaws, dark eyes and rounded "V" shape ears. Their tail is moderately thick and is carried horizontally when they are moving. The hair on their head and legs is short but longer on their muzzle, forming beard, eyebrows, ears, body and neck. Their coat color is russet gold. Wirehaired Vizslas are also expressive, gentle, loving, and trainable.

# Yorkshire Terrier

Yorkshire Terriers are small dogs nicknamed *Yokie* and developed during the 19th century in Yorkshire, England, to catch rats in clothing mills. They have a small head, black nose, dark eyes, V-shaped ears and straight legs with round feet and black toenails. Their long and glossy coat is fine and silky and falls straight down on either side. Their coat also comes in gray and tan color. The body and tail are gray and the rest of the dog is tan. On the other hand, puppies are brown, black and tan. The hair on their head is also extra thick and long. Yorkshire Terriers are very eager for adventure, highly energetic, brave, loyal and clever.

Images From: Ger Dekker, State Farm, Derek Key, Jerry Kirkhart, Maja Dumat, Jean, Julia Ballarin, Jamie Lantzy, Matt Batchelor, Jeffrey Beall, Svenska Mässan, Norm and Mary Kangas, Jon Mountjoy, carterse, Australian Silky Terrier Of Silky's Dream, CT M, fugzu, Andy Blackledge, mister b 1138, Daniel Flathagen, Katelyn, Petful, Mark Kimpel, Denis789, Seongbin Im, John Leslie, Grace, Corrado Dearca, Sendai Blog, Don Gunn, Sebastian Bulldog, Brad L., Roger Ahlbrand, annrhipublications, David Shankbone, David Sapeg, Prayitno / Thank you for (10 millions +) views, Tony Alter, Jaap Joris, localpups, Shelley Groomer, Scarlett2308, Pedro Lopez, Artur Malinowski, LEONARDO DASILVA, gomagoti, dutchmasterdutchie, Dirk Vorderstraße, Jean, Grete Stadlbauer, Guido Appenzeller, audrey_sel, Colin West, Silvia, Lil Shepherd, Ian Blacker, Jani Uusitalo, Kevin Rodriguez Ortiz, Bad Apple Photography, adam w, Andrea Arden, Thanate Tan, Andrew Hitchcock, Aljone, Anita Ritenour, Marauder Dawn, Brian Burger, woozie2010, meteo, Adam Singer, Robert Nunnally, Jena Fuller, M.Peinado, katsuuu 44, Cassie J, Don Richards, Kristin "Shoe" Shoemaker , Harold Meerveld, Rennett Stowe, Anvisuals, localpups/Flickr

Made in the USA
Columbia, SC
18 January 2020